HOW TO BECOME A
SUCCESSFUL RECRUITER

CAREER
CLINIC

CHAPTER 1

What makes a good recruiter?

What qualities distinguish a good recruiter? Good recruiters do more than just complete their daily tasks well. They make certain that their company consistently attracts and retains good employees. Recruiters do not have to have a background in human resources.

Good recruiting skills can be developed through experience in sales, design, marketing, customer service, coding, and a variety of other fields. Despite their varied backgrounds, there are a few characteristics that all hire-worthy recruiters should possess.

What is a recruiter purpose?

They are pros in attracting, finding, and screening candidates for open positions. From beginning to end, the hiring procedure is entirely under the recruiter's control. This can involve posting the job position, looking over resumes, conducting interviews, and collaborating with hiring managers to discover the best fit.

Recruiter Qualifications

Recruiters, contrary to popular belief, do not post jobs, wait for candidates to apply, interview them, and close the deal.

Entry Level Recruiter

Companies will hire an entry-level recruiter if they have at least two years of sales experience and a degree.

Type of recruiter

Corporate recruiters, retained recruiters, contingency recruiters, outplacement recruiters, and staffing agency recruiters are some of the diverse types of recruiters.

CHAPTER 2

Building Relationships

Building recruiter relationships does not imply using your resources whenever you need them. If you only contact people when you have a new job opening, your gesture will not appear genuine. Similarly, do not expect to get a good deal if you only call a contact when you are looking for one.

Spend time determining how you can assist your key business contacts. What value can you bring to the table to start the conversation?

Recruiters must reject more candidates than they hire, according to statistics. The best wat to do it gracefully, by transforming rejections into relationships. A post-interview rejection letter should be expected.

However, sending personalized emails and cultivating genuine relationships distinguishes good recruiters, even when they are rejecting candidates. A good recruiter recalls small, positive details from interactions

They also stay connected in case of future openings.

Reach out to different organizations:

Non-Profits Organizations

High Schools, Colleges, Post-Secondary, Technical Schools

Workforce Development

Unemployment Offices

Shelters

Returning Citizens

Radio Stations

with rejected applicants and uses them to personalize their messages. They highlight candidates' strengths and may even suggest other jobs for which they are qualified.

CHAPTER 3

Thinking Ahead

Recruiters who add value to their organization do not simply wait for a job posting announcement to begin looking for candidates. They've begun to build pipelines and maintain contact with previous applicants. They attract passive candidates and build a strong network.

They understand where to look for experienced candidates (such as GitHub for developers) and how to find new talent in unexpected places (like obscure Slack channels.) They aren't afraid to experiment with and benefit from social media recruiting. If they notice a department expanding, they collaborate with managers to forecast their hiring needs.

They attend HR events to stay current on hiring trends. HR is all about development, both for employees and for businesses, and a good recruiter keeps this in mind.

To post compelling job ads, good recruiters must be familiar with marketing techniques. They must function as salespeople. They should be familiar with psychology in order to better understand the reactions of candidates. Recruiters will also find themselves employing 'PR tricks' at recruitment events in order to improve their company's employer brand.

CHAPTER 4

Hiring Manger Relationship

Recruiters must sometimes navigate disagreements with hiring managers caused by conflicts of interest. A successful recruiter must figure out how to deal with these differences and balance the demands of hiring managers.

Everyone discusses candidate experience. However, hiring manager experience is also important. Keep in mind that hiring managers may not have enough time or knowledge to fully understand the hiring process. Good recruiters use their knowledge to draw attention to issues that hiring managers would overlook on their own, such as oblique indications that a candidate might turn out to be a future toxic coworker who undercuts their team. A good recruiter will also try to understand how each manager thinks. Because some hiring managers may want to choose between a few top candidates, recruiters should conduct in-depth screening interviews and ensure there are no critical deal-breakers afterward.

Another hiring manager may prefer to evaluate resumes on their own time. In this situation, a competent recruiter concentrates on finding qualified applicants and leaves the hiring manager in charge of screening and conducting interviews.

Here are some questions to ask:

What is the purpose of this position, and what value does it bring to the company?

Where is the job located?

Are you willing to consider remote candidates?

What is the pay scale, commission structure, and bonus structure?

Do you offer visa sponsorship?

What are the necessary qualifications for this position?

What are your desired qualifications for this position?

Can you describe the team's challenges? How will the candidate contribute to their resolution?

CHAPTER 5

Thinking Outside the Box

Effective recruiters understand that you should never judge a book by its cover or a candidate by their resume Unquestionably, a marketing manager can produce a strong resume, and a salesperson can portray themselves in the most interesting way.

But does this imply they are good at their job? Should a recruiter reject a developer with an improperly formatted resume?

Recruiters should look for evidence that candidates' skills match the job requirements by reading between the lines.

Qualified candidates can be identified using operational and behavioral interview questions. Recruiters could request specific information or assign projects to assess how their candidates manage job responsibilities.

More than that, recruiters who emphasize the importance of diversity over traditional requirements stand out. They recommend a candidate who they believe is enthusiastic enough to contribute innovative ideas to their team, even if they do not come from a stereotypical background.

Instead of hiring another "beer buddy," an effective recruiter will look for a candidate who is a "culture add" rather than a "culture fit."

CHAPTER 6

Nowadays, job searchers use social media to look for and apply for jobs. You must go where the people you want to hire are to get your positions in front of them. That includes the most popular social networks, such as LinkedIn, Facebook, and Twitter. Posting jobs on these platforms increases the visibility of your job postings among potential candidates.

We put together five creative ways to advertise job openings in the form of social media templates that you can easily customize to help you capture candidates' attention with informative and engaging posts.

LinkedIn

LinkedIn is the place to go to connect with both passive and active job candidates. You can post open positions on your website or share them with your network. Make the most of LinkedIn's paid job listings to advertise your open opportunities, connect with prospects, and reach the people you want to reach. To expedite the application process, you can also allow candidates to apply directly using information from their LinkedIn profiles.

A status update on your company's LinkedIn page is another effective way to promote a job opening. Include a quick link to the job posting or your company's career page. The followers and network of your company will see your job posting and may visit your careers page to learn more about it.

Facebook

Facebook is the most popular social network, posting jobs on Facebook allows you to reach many people. Employees, like LinkedIn, can share their company's new job opening and help reach even more job seekers.

Every company has its own culture and tone, but the following elements should be included in every Facebook job posting: the job title, the location, the benefits, and, of course, a call to action.

Twitter

You can also advertise your job openings on Twitter. Because of the character limit, only include what is necessary to attract qualified candidates' attention. Then, include a link to the complete job description, your careers page, or an application form. Make sure to include the job title, location, and a clear call to action in your Twitter job post.

If you want to share your job posting on social media, LinkedIn, Facebook, and Twitter are the best places to do so. However, there are numerous other platforms available, including more specialized social media for specific industries.

That is why we developed a generic 'We are hiring' social media post template. You can use it on any social channel you believe will assist you in attracting and finding new candidates and future employees. Also, here are some general guidelines to follow when posting a job on social media:

Make it clear that this is a job posting.

Include critical information.

Emphasize your company's culture.

Keep your post brief.

CHAPTER 7

Sourcing for Candidates

Sourcing is the process of locating and qualifying candidates, both passive and active, who have not applied directly to an open position. You are looking for information on sourced candidates such as their names, qualifications, and contact information. There are numerous sourcing tools available. Artificial intelligence is currently one of the most exciting technologies.

For sourcing, AI provides two major advantages: automation and accuracy.

Automated sourcing employs technology to locate candidates online who meet the requirements of your position. This can involve searching specifically within resume databases like CareerBuilder or general web scraping for applicants. The time it takes to fill a position and the cost of hiring should both decrease as automation in applicant sourcing increases.

The other genuine advantage of AI for sourcing is the ability to improve candidate matching accuracy. Instead of limited and error-prone keyword and Boolean searches, AI can detect patterns in resumes and other data sources to identify candidates who are better matches for a job's requirements.

CHAPTER 8

Recruiter Call

A recruiter call, also known as a phone interview, is a conversation that helps a company learn more about you as a candidate. This conversation usually takes place at the start of the hiring process and includes questions about your experience, skills, and qualifications. Incorporating this stage into hiring processes can assist companies in identifying candidates to interview in person. Some candidates use these calls to ask questions about the company or the position.

Make it your job to ensure that the resume you send is accurate and free of gaps, errors, and inconsistencies. Discuss all the crucial points with your client ahead and emphasize those that are important because this candidate reflects your judgment. Tell the applicant to revise the resume and include any modifications you recommend. A resume is a significant piece of writing. Recruiters must make sure this is as fantastic as it can be. If all you are doing is shifting papers around, aren't you just managing the hiring process? not having any impact. As you are all aware, hiring managers will not consider unprofessional resumes. It is the recruiter's responsibility to ensure this is not the case.

Here are questions to ask:

Can you tell me about your background?

Why are you looking for a new job?

Where are you in your job search?

When could you start working?

How much would you like to earn in this position?

Are there specific benefits that are important to you?

Would it be a deal breaker for you if we do not offer _______ (benefit) or the salary figure you quoted?

What skills have you recently gained or strengthened?

How are your skills a match for this job?

What did you do during the yearlong gap in your employment (and why did you leave your last employer)?

What questions do you have for me?

CHAPTER 9

Presenting the Applicant to the Hiring Manager

Even if you only interview candidates over the phone, you should still evaluate each one formally and submit your findings. Even a basic interview should include a thorough examination of the applicant's work history and a brief evaluation of their most noteworthy achievements. Be careful to take thorough notes. These must include a description of the actual outcomes obtained, illustrations of significant characteristics, and an evaluation of crucial job-related variables. I recommend grading the candidate on one-to-five scale for each of the essential qualities (some examples include motivation, ability, team skill, cultural fit, and trend of progress) using a formal evaluation template. This official evaluation proves that the recruiter conducted a competent and fair evaluation. After that, the recruiting manager will usually perform an equally thorough evaluation using your ratings as a benchmark. You will come across as a professional the moment you submit these documents as a package with your formal presentation. Some people might think this requires too much effort.

However, cutting back on send outs by 50% to 100% for each task will allow you plenty time to assemble the package. It will only take you 30 minutes for each candidate once you get the process down.

Therefore, investing an hour in this procedure will save you eight to twelve hours spent looking for more candidates for a task that, by all rights, ought to have been finished sooner. You will be able to identify better candidates for each job or work on additional assignments with the net 10+ hours you will save. In the process, you will gain the recognition you merit for a job well done in a professional manner. The formal presentation package I suggest is made to guard against common hiring mistakes and everyday issues. We have found that with a little foresight, many mistakes committed throughout the hiring process can be easily avoided. Recruiters can miss vital details. Interviews are typically cursory and conducted by hiring managers. Everybody has bias. There is never enough time. A team member who is having a terrible day or is a poor interviewer can be given assignments. In the process, you'll gain the recognition you merit for a job well done in a professional manner.

A strong candidate can be disqualified with just one "no" decision based on a shallow or erroneous evaluation. Most of these issues are resolved before they have a chance to arise with a comprehensive presentation package. The formal presentation and presenting procedure I provide demonstrates unequivocally that the recruiter has conducted thorough and accurate assessment. This dispels the widespread misconception held by many managers that recruiters merely pre-screen resumes. Giving proof of actual skill changes the hiring manager interview's primary goal. The question is no longer whether a candidate is a possibility but whether they are one of the finalists. This is a surefire way to reduce the number of send outs. The recruiter has done all the demanding work and is now seen as a critical piece of the hiring puzzle, not just someone submitting resumes. When your clients believe that every candidate you recommend has a 50/50 chance of getting hired, you will be thanked for a job well done. You will deserve it.

CHAPTER 10

Make the Offer

At first look, the procedure for sending a job offer to a candidate could seem straightforward: you draft the offer letter, request management approval, and then send it to potential employees. But each of these demands time, energy, a lot of cooperation, and careful consideration.

Here are some pointers to help you streamline the job offer procedure:

To whom does this position report?
It is possible that the team leader and hiring manager are not the same individual.

What is the range of salary for this job?
For this information, consult the wage structure of your organization.

What factors will determine the final compensation package?
You might choose to pay applicants with more education or experience more money.

Are there any bonuses associated with this position?
Talk about additional pay, such as commissions, bonuses, and prizes.

What sort of advantages will we provide?
For instance, you might provide senior roles with stock options and other positions with training possibilities.

How long should we wait before accepting a candidate's offer?
Ideally, prospects will accept in a few of days at most, but you using your initial criteria as a guide expedites the process once you have chosen your top candidate. You may need to go over all these again if your finalist tries to bargain.

CHAPTER 11

Offer Letter Templates

When creating offers, an offer letter template can save you a lot of time. All that is required of you, or members of your hiring team is that you fill in the blanks with details particular to each position.

Additionally, a well-crafted template will assist you in ensuring that you cover all the crucial aspects of the position and greet every new hire in the appropriate manner.

We created the following template, which is free to use and simple to adapt to your business needs:

Dear

We are pleased to offer you a job as a [role title] at [company name]. We think that your experience and skills will be a valuable asset to our company.

If you accept this offer, you will be eligible for the following, in accordance with our company's policies:

Annual gross salary of $[total annual salary] paid in [monthly or semi-monthly] installments by check or direct deposit

Up to [percent]% of your annual gross salary as a performance bonus

Standard benefits including:

[vacation days number] days of annual paid time off

[sick days number] days of sick leave

Medical and dental insurance

401k/retirement plan

Flexible working hours

Tuition reimbursement for career development courses

Childcare

[more benefits]

Sign this letter as shown below, date it, and email it back to us by [date] to accept this offer. Your anticipated start date is [date]. [Supervisor's name] will be your direct report. We look forward to welcoming you to our team. Feel free to call [recruiter's name] if you have any questions or concerns.

Sincerely,

Signatures:

Company Representative (Sign)

Date

Applicant (Sign)

Date

When: Extending employment offers to applicants without the aid of an automated system takes time.

Team members and I exchange a lot of emails back and forth to ensure that the offer letter is approved. Make sure your offer letter is flawless, interesting, and consistent with your brand. You must track applicants' responses and demand tracking.

To follow up with team members or candidates, you need a quick and accurate overview of who has acted and who hasn't. To keep everything in one place for quick access, you need a system.

The email you send to applicants informing them of your offer. To add in your template, pick from a selection of variables like "candidate name" and "position." The information that corresponds to each applicant will be automatically substituted for these variables in your email.

The official offer letter, which must be signed by applicants and contains all the job specifics. Workable lets you customize your own offer letter template by uploading it. Placeholders for significant variables like "salary," "direct manager," and "offer expiration date" should be included. Workable will automatically change the placeholders in the official document when it's time to establish a new offer; just enter the pertinent information for each candidate in the boxes provided.

Set approvers for offer letters. They will be notified by Workable to accept and sign your offer letter. Workable will immediately email the cover letter to the candidate after it has been accepted.

Enabling e-signatures from team members and candidates will hasten the process.

Easily keep track of offer letter rejections from candidates and members of the team. Rejecting parties can also make comments stating their reasons.

Since it can be difficult to find the ideal candidate, streamlining your job offer procedure will ensure that you have everything you need to recruit quickly. Templates, approval workflows, and e-signature features let you communicate effectively and quickly, enabling you to provide satisfying experiences that encourage your finest applicants to work for your organization.

1

CHAPTER 12

Rejecting candidates? Call them!

Even though sending or receiving a rejection email or call may not be enjoyable, it will make a positive impression on applicants you might wish to consider for future positions. Here are some guidelines to help you politely reject candidates:

Make your rejection emails specific to the hiring step. After the screening process, if you decide not to hire an applicant, use succinct but respectful remarks.

Personalize your emails to those who made it to the end of your employment process to keep the lines of communication open.

Answer inquiries regarding interview feedback. Inform candidates of your decision if they request comments on their interview.

To prevent legal issues, stick to job-related criteria and, if appropriate, recommend staying connected for additional relevant employment vacancies in.

CHAPTER 13

Helping with Onboarding

Although the recruiting manager and human resources often manage the bulk of the onboarding, you can aid candidates in making a smooth transition from applicant to employee. This is how:

The employee's information into your HRIS. Or give the human resources department the specifics of new hires (such as their contact information, starting date, etc.) so they may update their internal databases.

Inform the staff of the new hire. Send an email with a new hire announcement to employees to let them know about their new coworker. Make sure the IT department sets up the new hire's software accounts, as necessary. Additionally, contact accounting to get your new hire added to payroll.

After the first week and month, schedule a meeting with newly hired employees. Ask them how they are settling into the job, whether it meets their expectations, and for suggestions on how to make future hiring procedures better.

CHAPTER 14

Examine hiring metrics.

Time to hire and source of hiring KPIs in recruiting might highlight areas for improvement: Act in response to trends Metrics tracking alone is insufficient. Data should be interpreted and used in ways that are appropriate for your hiring strategy. For instance, if you observe that one sourcing channel attracts more

Instructive. Examine the feedback candidates leave regarding your hiring procedure.

qualified candidates than others, recommend readjusting your recruitment budget. **Think about candidate-related metrics as well.** Online evaluations and questionnaires about the hiring process might also be

CHAPTER 15

Stay Positive

There is no such thing as a terrible experience for good recruiters. Making mistakes teaches us important things. When they do not get the outcomes, they were hoping for, they investigate what went wrong and how to fix it moving forward. They rejoice over both minor and major accomplishments, such as a prompt hire or securing a candidate for an open position.

But they also look for methods to get better all the time. They must keep up with all recent HR advancements if they want to stay ahead of the competition.

How can HR technology boost employees' productivity?

What are the most current trends in hiring?

What are the best techniques for recruiting on social media?

How are they changing their sourcing practices?

These are the queries that successful recruiters ask themselves.

Here are some companies that hire Junior Recruiters:

ConsultNet

Weston & Sampson

Randstad

Kelly Services

Kelly Connect

Sustainable Talent

RemX

Aston Health

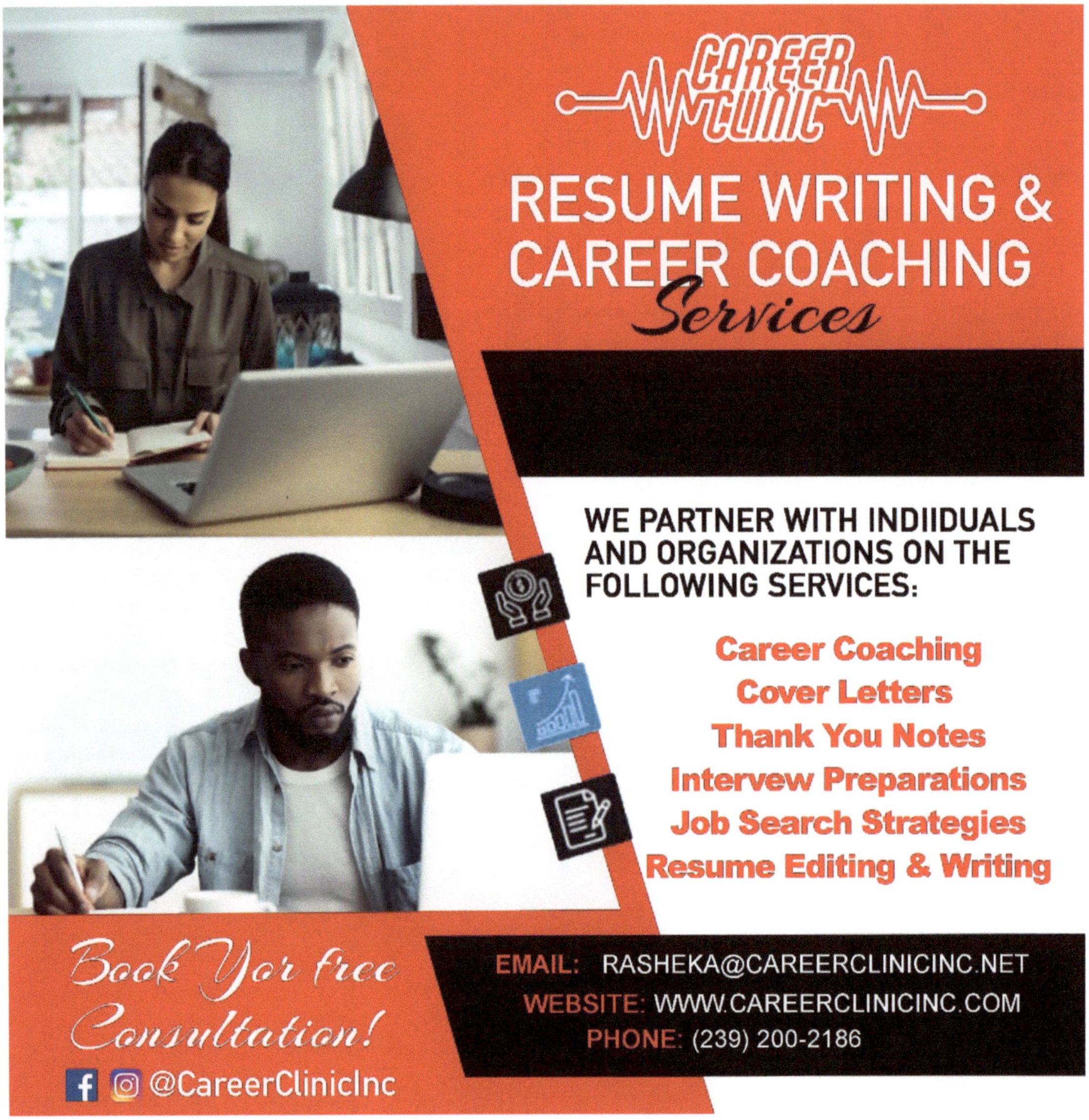
CAREER CLINIC
RESUME WRITING &
CAREER COACHING
Services
WE PARTNER WITH INDIIDUALS AND ORGANIZATIONS ON THE FOLLOWING SERVICES:
Career Coaching
Cover Letters
Thank You Notes
Intervew Preparations
Job Search Strategies
Resume Editing & Writing
Book Yor free Consultation!
@CareerClinicInc
EMAIL: RASHEKA@CAREERCLINICINC.NET
WEBSITE: WWW.CAREERCLINICINC.COM
PHONE: (239) 200-2186

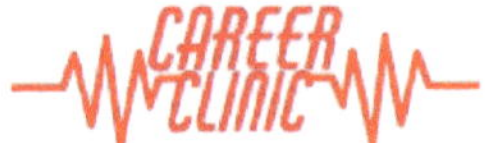

Time to Start Recruiting Good Luck!!